MAN OF DESTINY

By

Stephen Kato

Published by

The Transparent Publishing Company

www.TransparentPublishing.co.uk

ISBN Paperback 9781909805309

ISBN eBook 9781909805316

First published October 2015

Original Copyright holder – ©Stephen Kato

Cover Photography by Peter Ribbeck

www.PeterRibbeck.com

Unless otherwise stated all Scriptures quoted are from King James Version

CONTENTS

PAGE

CHAPTER 1 - EVERY IMPACT HAS A SOURCE

"And, behold, a certain lawyer stood up, and tempted him, saying, Master, what shall I do to inherit eternal life?
He said unto him, What is written in the law? How readest thou?
And he answering said, Thou shalt love the Lord thy God with all thy heart, and with all thy soul, and with all thy strength, and with all thy mind; and thy neighbour as thyself.
And he said unto him, Thou hast answered right: this do, and thou shalt live.
But he, willing to justify himself, said unto Jesus, And who is my neighbour?
And Jesus answering said, A certain man went down from Jerusalem to Jericho, and fell among thieves, which stripped him of his raiment, and wounded him, and departed , leaving him half dead.
And by chance there came down a certain priest that way: and when he saw him, he passed by on the other side.
And likewise a Levite, when he was at the place, came and looked on him, and passed by on the other side.
But a certain Samaritan, as he journeyed, came where he was: and when he saw him, he had compassion on him.
And went to him, and bound up his wounds, pouring in oil and wine, and set him on his own beast, and brought him to an inn, and took care of him.
And on the morrow when he departed, he took out two pence, and gave them to the host, and said unto him, Take care of him; and whatsoever thou spendest more, when I come again, I will repay thee.
Which now of these three, thinkest thou, was neighbour unto him that fell among the thieves?
And he said, He that shewed mercy on him.
Then said Jesus unto him, Go, and do thou likewise." Luke 10:25-37

This story of the Good Samaritan as we all know it is one of the most impactful stories that has ever been told in the world today. The name Good Samaritan is used by many organisations, schools, shops, hospitals and nursery schools.

It is a story carrying a great message, impacting lives regardless of age, religion, race or, gender. Everyone wants to be a "Good Samaritan!" Every well intentioned act could be described as a Good Samaritan act.

After discovering the impact that the good Samarian has had on myself and the world-at-large, I felt a lot of questions about the same that needed a lot of answers:

- Why does the Good Samaritan story have so much impact compared to other stories?
- Why is the story so famous to everyone, both young and old?
- Why is it so powerful to all religions?
- Can we learn more from it?
- Is it just a story or is there something more in it?
- How can it relate to our life today?

The Spirit of the Lord began to deal with my heart and gave me insight and revelations that are going to help you so much in your life as you read this book.

The same verse 30 that we used to begin with reading this story started to bring another meaning to me. The verse begins,

And Jesus answering said, A certain man went down.

Now even before I finished reading this verse I heard the Spirit of God telling me to read it again, "And Jesus answering, said". He said read again! "And Jesus answering said." When I read it about five or six times my eyes got opened and I saw that THE STORY OF THE GOOD SAMARITAN IS AN ANSWER!
"Jesus answering," - it was an answer.

Answers Make Impact

Everything on earth that creates impact on earth has a source and a foundation. I have come to discover that answers make impact. Answers are loved by everybody. Answers are known and witnessed by everyone. The wrong questions can rob us of the joy of salvation, but the right questions reveal a reason for the glory of God to be made known in our lives. When you live a life of answers, you will be known to everyone. The whole world hears about you. They all want to associate with you. Young and old alike love you. Answers make impact!

But remember you cannot get an answer when you have no question. The question comes before an answer. Many people love answers and hate questions yet you can't get answers without questions. They love fruits and hate roots. At school the teachers used to say the roots of education are bitter but its fruits are the sweetest. It is the bitter than will lead you to the sweeter.

Apostle Paul writes to the Romans,
"For I reckon that the sufferings of this present time are not worthy to be compared with the glory which shall be revealed in us." Romans 8:18

This just confirms that for you to get in a place of glory, you must have gone through some sufferings. Sufferings now become your transport to the glory. All people that are living the best life today have gone through real struggles. Before you admire their impact, please ask them about where they are coming from and about the things they have gone through.

Now back to the story of the Good Samaritan. If it's an answer as we can see, where is the question? I found it in verse 25,
"And, behold, a certain lawyer stood up, and tempted him, saying, Master, what shall I do to inherit eternal life?"
This is the question.

But when you look at this question you might think the lawyer is looking for eternal life, yet when you consider it properly you will find that behind his question there is the motive of why it is being asked. When the verse says "… *and tempted him.*" This lawyer had another reason why he asked this question. He was not looking for the answer to it. That's why the writer of the bible doesn't give us his name but his profession (lawyer). His name is not important because everyone has a name. But his profession is significant because not everyone has a profession and his was not just a common profession but a great one. A lawyer can cause the guilty to be found not guilty and the not guilty to be found guilty.

He stood up to "tempt" or "test" Jesus. He wanted to play around with the thinking capacity of Jesus; to measure his reasoning competence. The very question he asked as he tempted Jesus became the foundation of this Scripture. His question became the source of the story of the Good Samaritan as we know it.

Jesus decided to prove to him that he was a creature and He is Creator. He was clay and Jesus is the Potter. How can the creature tempt the Creator and how can clay tempt the Potter? The man was trying to tempt Jesus by asking him a question. Jesus answered him with another question and put the man in a position whereby as he answers Jesus' question, he will be answering his own question which he has just asked. When you ask someone a question and he answers you with a question, such that the answer to his question is the answer to your question, then that person is more intelligent than you!

After this lawyer saw that Jesus had shamed him on the first question, he had again to ask a second question. Remember the first question was, "*What shall I do to inherit eternal life?*" Then the second question is now, "*Who is my neighbour?*" This question gave rise to Jesus answering with the story of the Good Samaritan.

Testing/Temptation gives birth to Revelation

It was through this temptation that the lawyer tempted Jesus causing Him to get a revelation of the Good Samaritan story. You can believe together with me that if Jesus would not have been tempted by this lawyer, he couldn't have spoken this story.

Therefore, the story of the Good Samaritan is a product of a temptation. It was this temptation that gave birth to the revelation. Did you know that without a temptation, there will rarely be a revelation? Throughout all history, people who have encountered those "lawyers" i.e. temptations and tests and stand, have come up with products of revelation that have changed their lives and the lives of those who learned about them. We remember them, read about them, and learn from them because of the tests and temptations they went through.

I know I am talking to someone going through a lot of tests and temptations. Many "lawyers" have stood to ask you a lot of questions. You have a lot of questions in your business, in your marriage, in your relationships and questions about your future. All these questions are not for nothing. God allows them to come in order for you to get answers called revelations.

Every time you face a situation in your life that creates a lot of questions, don't make easy conclusions before you ask God why and be patient as you wait for the answer from God. It might take longer than you expected but always reason on God's side. Many times God has revealed Himself to his people through challenges. God has used these tests to prove himself faithful to his people. He has introduced himself to many through challenges.

Take an example of people like Jacob. God allowed him to run out of his father's house, take a journey to Haran thinking maybe life is not fair to him. He was full of questions in heart, but even before he got to the end of his journey God showed up and introduced himself to him when he was sleeping on a stone.

After Jacob was blessed by his father Isaac (remember it was his mother Rebecca who led him by force to tap into that blessing and then because of that a lot of problems and troubles and death threats from his brother followed); Jacob had a lot of questions that needed answers. However at this very point of time, on the way, is when God speaks to Jacob through a dream and gives him all the answers that he needed. The Bible says:

"And Jacob went out from Beersheba, and went toward Haran. And he lighted upon a certain place, and tarried there all night, because the sun was set; and he took of the stones of that place, and put them for his pillows, and lay down in that place to sleep. And he dreamed, and behold a ladder set up on the earth, and the top of it reached to heaven: and behold the angels of God ascending and descending on it. And behold, the Lord stood above it, and said, I am the Lord God of Abraham thy father, and the God of Isaac: the land whereon thou liest, to thee will I give it, and to thy seed.

And thy seed shall be as many as the dust of the earth, and thou shalt spread abroad to the west, and to the east, and to the north, and to the south: and in thee and in thy seed shall all the families of the earth be blessed. And, behold, I am with thee and will keep thee in all places whither thou goest, and will bring thee again into this land; for I will not leave thee, until I have done that which I have spoken to thee of. And Jacob awakened out of his sleep, and he said, Surely the Lord is in this place; and I knew it not." Genesis 28:10-16 KJV

The message that God gave to Jacob was exactly like the one that his father spoke to him when he was blessing him. Even although his mother Rebecca had intervened and manoeuvred for Jacob to receive the blessing that his father intended for his brother, nonetheless Jacob saw that God's plan was exactly what his mother had foresaw. What amazes me is that

God couldn't speak to Jacob when he was still in his father's house. He waited until he gets out, and sleeps on stones! Can you imagine? God will always take you out of your comfort zone for Him to speak to you.

A young man with a father and mother alive with all the riches and servants in the house, is now sleeping on stones away very far from home. Isn't that a big test? But through this test God showed up in his life.

There are some of you who think, right now, you should have been somewhere "home" but it's like the distance from where you are, to where you are supposed to be is too long and you are tired and complaining so much. Listen to me, God has separated you for just a moment so that He may deliver a certain message to you.

What you have to know is that you are not sleeping on these stones forever. You shall not sleep in those rental houses forever. You shall not work for other people forever. You shall not be barren forever. Many people have gone through such and they are now in their rightful places. You will not be the first one to die there. The same God who helped others, will help you also.

The same Jacob became the great nation that God had promised Abraham. ALL the fame and the impact that Jacob (now Israel) has is everlasting. Everyone knows him. The whole world knows Israel.

Joseph the Dreamer

Look at this young man Joseph, a great dreamer - having his immense destiny revealed to him by God through dreams, yet not knowing that it will cost him quite a lot.

We all know how his brothers hated him because of the dreams and later sold him to the Midianites, and the Midianites to Potiphar and Potiphar's wife wanted to rape him and later changed the story against Joseph, and they threw him in prison, then from this prison we see Joseph becoming the first Prime Minister of Egypt after interpreting Pharaoh's dream. He became a very great man who made a tremendous impact in the whole world.

These kind of tests and temptations that Joseph went through made him what he became. It's these rough roads that lead us to the right places in life. I like his testimony to his brother. Joseph says,

"So now it was not you that sent me hither, but God: and he hath made me a father to Pharaoh, and lord of all his house, and a ruler throughout all the land of Egypt." Genesis 45:8 (KJV)

Joseph says in the Scriptures, *"it was not you that sent me here but God."* In other words, God will always use people to get people to their great destiny. But these people that God will use will be always releasing tests and temptations to us. Begin to thank God for all those who are standing against you today. Don't even look up to them, look up to God because without them we cannot get to the fulfilment of our dreams. Their negative contribution sends us to our positive destination.

Dreamers are always hated. God always wants them never to settle for less, but to pursue their dreams until they get fulfilled in their lives.

It's always possible to get settled in wrong places. If you don't have some "lawyers" asking you many questions, so the challenges help us to wake up. When your time to go to the never level or class comes, tests will always come first before a new class. It has to be the examination paper that will approve us for the next class.

CHAPTER 2 - TEST IS THE PRICE FOR PROMOTION

We all pray and trust God for our classes to change but God will not promote someone that He has not proved. You must qualify first. No one can qualify to drive a car if he/she has not passed the driving test. It is the test that qualifies people.

Every testing season in your life is not a bad season, it's the best season because it comes to promote you to the next level in your life. Oh my God! After what you are going through right now, you shall be promoted in Jesus' name. Say amen! That challenge is not going to leave you weaker but it will make you stronger. It shall not leave you in the same place it found you. It is your ladder to your next level in Jesus' name.

Daniel, Shadrach, Meshach and Abed-nego

Daniel, Shadrach, Meshach and Abed-nego in Babylon became a great example to us as we talk about these tests that we always go through in life. I was looking at their lives and how God promoted them in a foreign land. In the second chapter of the book of Daniel, you will discover how Daniel was promoted after passing the test of interpreting the dream of King Nebuchadnezzar. The last three verses of that second chapter say:

The king answered unto Daniel, and said, Of a truth it is, that your God is a God of gods, and a lord of Kings, and a revealer of secrets, seeing thou couldest reveal this secret.
Then the king made Daniel a great man, and gave him many great gifts, and made him ruler over the whole province of Babylon, and chief of the governors over all the wise men of Babylon.

Then Daniel requested of the king , and he set Shadrach, Meshach, and Abed-nego, over the affairs of the province of

Babylon: but Daniel sat in the gate of the king." Daniel 2:47-49 (KJV)

When I was looking at these three verses, I came to discover that one man here, Daniel, is the one who had interpreted the dream of the king and only this one man Daniel was promoted by the king. And in the last verse (v49) we read how he requests the king to promote his brothers as well. Now remember that these brothers had never been tested for this promotion; they are getting it by the request of Daniel.

What surprises me is that the following chapter three, the price of their rightful promotion begins to cook up. The golden image is set up, and everyone, every tribe and nationality must bow and worship this image of gold. And these three men refuse. I was asking myself where was Daniel in this chapter. Does it mean that Daniel bowed down and worshipped the golden image? The answer is no. But this wasn't all about Daniel. It was now all about these three men. These three must pay a price for their promotion.

When God is out to promote you, you will feel as though every challenge is just directing itself to you. This is the point when you find people asking themselves, "Why me?" When you try to look at others, they are not passing through what you are passing through. I am here to let you know that there is a new level calling you. There is a promotion after that. God wouldn't allow you to go through that if he was not taking you somewhere better.

Daniel was not mentioned in this whole chapter. The entire chapter was just about Shadrach, Meshach and Abed-nego. What do you do when the whole chapter is all about you? When everybody is talking about you? The whole church, community, company is talking about you.

They were famous in all the newspapers on the front page. All the provinces read and heard about them. The king left every programme that he had and dealt with these accordingly. He commanded the furnace to be kindled more than seven times hotter. People left their businesses and they came to witness these three stubborn men die in the furnace. These three men had the audacity to think that they could change the commandment of the king. These three men stood up for the only true God they worshipped, who was viewed as simply another God in Babylon.

Negatives are Stepping Stones to our Positive Future

They came from all over to witness these three men. I always like it when I see God using the negatives we go through as stepping stones to positive future.

The king and all his men and the whole kingdom witnessed these three men bound and thrown in the furnace of fire. The very people who threw them into the fire were burned to death. But the king himself witnessed that these three men were not harmed by the fire and he saw another man with them in the furnace, whom he says is like the Son of God. The king called them out of the furnace and people came to witness the men whom fire could not harm.

In the last three verses of chapter three of Daniel's book, the king says,

"Then Nebuchadnezzar spake, and said, Blessed be the God of Shadrach, Meshach and Abed-nego, who hath sent his angel, and delivered his servants that trusted in him, and have changed the king's word, and yielded their bodies, that they might not serve nor worship any god, except their own God.

Therefore I make a decree, That every people, nation, and language, which speak anything amiss against the God of Shadrach, Meshach, and Abed-nego, shall be cut in pieces, and their houses shall be made a dunghill: because there is no other God that can deliver after this sort.

Then the king promoted Shadrach, Meshach, and Abed-nego, in the province of Babylon." Daniel 3:28-30 (KJV)

Remember in the preceding chapter two, Daniel is the one who was promoted and in the last verse Daniel requested the promotion of Shadrach, Meshach and Abed-nego. But in the following chapter three, the king promotes these three men himself. What I am trying to say is that the promotion, "requested for" and the promotion, "paid for" are two different promotions.

The promotion "requested for" even when you are promoted, you will not be honoured; But the promotion "paid for", even when you are promoted you shall be honoured forever.

The ending of these two chapters amazes me. One ends when Daniel is the one promoted and the other ends when the three men are promoted. In this I learn not to be offended by the promotion of my brother, because I know just as he is promoted in one chapter, I will also be promoted in the next chapter.

Stop looking negatively at the promotion of others, as if they are the last one to be promoted. God who promoted them is the same God who will promote you as well. Don't look at the chapter that has ended without your promotion as being the final chapter. There must be another chapter that shall end after you are promoted. I see your chapter coming.

After all these people in Babylon witnessed the men of God that fire couldn't harm, they were promoted without challenge. When those who have opposed you hear you have been promoted and gone through trial by fire no one will ever desire to challenge you in that office because they will know what it took for you to obtain that blessing.

When they look at the kind of price you paid to get there, they will be careful with you. Competition comes where a cheap price has been paid. What you get cheaply, everyone will desire for it. When you see something everybody is running for, then you must know it is very cheap. It's always the few that have access to expensive things, because it's always these few that are ready to pay the price.

Many people desire to be great in life, but few are ready to pay the price to be great. Greatness is not a product of desire, but it is a product of the price paid. The price you are ready to pay will always determine the kind of life you shall live. You will always live within the parameters of your price.

I will always desire to have what I have paid for, or what I am ready to pay for. I will not aspire for something that I cannot afford to pay for. Anything that is beyond my ability to pay is beyond my reach. But if I can pay for it, then I can have it.

CHAPTER 3 - TEMPTATION LEADS TO REVELATION

The question that the lawyer asked as he tempted Jesus caused the Lord to get a revelation of the Good Samaritan story.

On this very point I want to say that the questions that you have now concerning your life, marriage, future etc. God has allowed them because they are going to help you to get revelations of the same. I have seen how such questions have helped people to tap into the supernatural after they were asked. There is a time in the Scriptures where Jesus Himself asked his disciples:

When Jesus came into the Coasts of Caesarea Philippi, he ASKED his disciples, saying, Whom do men say that I the Son of Man am? And they said, Some say that thou art John the Baptist: Some Elias; and others, Jeremias, or one of the prophets.
He saith unto them, But whom say ye that I am?
And Simon Peter answered and said, Thou art the Christ, the Son of the Living God.
And Jesus answered and said unto him, Blessed art thou, Simon Bar-jona: for flesh and blood hath not REVEALED it unto thee, but my Father which is in heaven.
And I say unto thee, That thou are Peter, and upon this rock I will build my church; and the gates of hell shall not prevail against it.
And I will give unto thee the keys of the kingdom of heaven: and whatsoever thou shalt bind on earth shall be bound in heaven: And whatsoever thou shalt loose on earth shalt be loosed in heaven. Matthew 16:13-19 (KJV)

We can see in these Scriptures what happened to Peter after Jesus asked a question. Jesus tells Peter 'this has not been REVEALED to you by flesh or blood but my father in heaven." Do you see that word' REVEALED'? Revelation comes to

Peter from heaven AFTER Jesus asked a question. What is revelation? It simply means : A manifestation of divine truth when the hidden comes to be known. This means that there are so many manifestations of divine truth that we fall short of every time we run away from questions. Questions provoke our Father in heaven to speak. The truth about you will never be revealed until questions have been asked to you and of you. Those questions that people always raise about your future provoke heaven to release the divine truth about your future.

The problem we have in our days is that people take questions negatively. But I want you to know that negative questions can bring positive answers. They ask negatively as they tempt us, yet, the same temptation opens our door to divine manifestations. Oh I love this!

That is why when God is ready to talk to you more, He will allow you to go to a place where many questions will be raised. He will allow you to meet more and bigger challenges that will help you to raise more questions. Of course, you can't sleep on those questions, like: Will you make it in this journey? Or like Jacob, do you think your mother Rebecca played with your future? What are you going to do? Are you sure you will live after this? Will you not die of hunger? Will you get to your destiny destination?

I mean many, many questions will come up. Every time you face a challenge like David and Goliath. This is when David was asked so many questions. Will you be able to fight that man? Why have you come here? Whom have you left the few sheep with? Don't you think you are dying today? Can you make it? Isn't your pride killing you? Can't you see you're too young? I mean countless questions will always rise up. But the good news is how God steps in with answers that are outstanding, speaking and revealing destiny in a very special way and manifesting divine truth concerning your life. As they all watch they will see God proving himself in you. They will witness how God is defending you and fighting for you putting down all your risen challenges. I pray that this will happen to you in Jesus' name. You will not fail and you will not fall in the hands of your enemies in Jesus' name.

It doesn't matter how long you have been in that place of challenges and opposition. God is coming to your rescue. They all watched you face it, they shall also watch you come out of it. God is going to surprise you this year. He is going to change your position. He is going to put a new song in your heart. Get ready for a new testimony, you are rising to the next level in Jesus' name.

You cannot hear heaven speak to you and your level remains the same. That's impossible. I mean, when God speaks to you, you must get to the next level.

After God revealed who Jesus was to Peter and Peter answered the question of Jesus and said, '*You are the Christ the Son of the Living God,*' immediately Jesus separated Peter from the others and began to talk to him alone: *You are Peter, and upon this rock I will build my church and the gates of hell shall not prevail against it. And I will give unto thee the keys of the Kingdom ….*

Now Jesus is not speaking all this to all the disciples. No, he is speaking to Peter alone. Why? Because he is the one who heard God speak. He is the only one who had a revelation. This is where revelation now becomes very important. It's the qualification to keys of the Kingdom. You can only access the keys of the Kingdom through revelation. When you get the keys, you can now bind and loose whatever on earth and heaven will respond accordingly. You will have the power and the authority to remove and replace the demonic ruling powers in your family. Every governing force that opposes the will of God will be subject to your authority in Christ. You will cause a revolution in your place. It's the "temptation" that will introduce you to the revelation, and revelation introduces you to the revolution.

Anybody who stands and overcomes temptations will always live a life full of revelations. And anybody who lives by revelations will always cause revolutions everywhere he/she goes.

All those who have composed songs often testify about the challenges, tests and temptations that they went through before they got the revelation of that song. Every song composed often has a very bad story behind it.

Powerful preachers and ministers of the Gospel all have stories to tell. Even the one who wrote the book of Revelation, he has a story to tell of how he was thrown onto the Island called Patmos. Even writers of books must go through some difficult things in order for them to write from a deep place of revelation and grace.

I have some good news for you. After all that you are going through people shall read your book. You are coming out with a book. They shall read about the lions and bears that you fought; the Goliaths that you defeated; the den of lions they threw you in; the furnace of fire you went through; the Red seas that you crossed; the bitter water that you drunk; the battles that you waged and even the rental houses that you slept in. All these heroes of the faith that we read about and those that we have witnessed with our very eyes, the list is endless. You cannot mention them all. But what blesses me is that the list has not ended yet. You are also going to show up on the same list of those who overcome. Your generation must read about you. It's not in vain for you to go through what you are going through. Remember, so many people are watching you from a distance. They want to know what will really happen to you next.

They are following you from a distance. Your victory will be their victory and your failure will be their disappointment. But I have prayed for you, in the name of Jesus Christ of Nazareth, you shall come out a winner. Victory is on your side. Say Amen!

Your Victory Shall also be their Victory

You shall become an example to many. They shall be proud of you. You will be an encouragement to them. You will become their adviser. That's why the children of Israel on their journey from Egypt, when they were crossing the Jordan river, received these words of divine instruction from God,

And it came to pass, when all the people were clean passed over Jordan, that the Lord spake unto Joshua saying,

Take you twelve men out of the people, out of every tribe a man. And command ye them, saying, Take you hence out of the midst of Jordan, out of the place where the priests' feet stood firm, twelve stones, and yet shall carry them over with you, and leave them in the lodging place, where ye shall lodge this night. Then Joshua called the twelve men, whom he had prepared of the children of Israel, out of every tribe a man: And Joshua said unto them, Pass over before the ark of the Lord your God into the midst of the Jordan, and take ye up every man of you a stone upon his shoulder, according unto the number of the tribes of the children of Israel: That this may be a sign among you, that when your children ask their fathers in time to come, saying, What mean ye by these stones?
Then ye shall answer them, That the waters of Jordan were cut off before the ark of the covenant of the Lord; when it passed over Jordan, the waters of Jordan were cut off: and these stones shall be for a memorial unto the children of Israel forever." Joshua 4:1-7 (KJV)

God himself had to command that these twelve stones should be collected right from the midst of the Jordan, as a memorial forever to the people that will come after. This was to stand as an everlasting victory, that all the children to come would always see it and know their God is able. What he did to others who came before, he can do the same even to those who come after. So the victory that you are going to have is not only for you, but for those who will come after you also.

The reason why you feel the challenge is too heavy for you to bear alone is because it is not for you alone. You are fighting for yourself and for your next generation. You are laying foundations for the next generation as well. Some things have to be remembered about you as a testimony: he/she was the first one to be born again in the whole family; the first one to preach the Gospel; the first one to drive a car. He/she was the first one to introduce that idea, faith, belief in God here.

It's not easy for you because you must first of all destroy what has been there as a wrong foundation, and again build what is supposed to be there. But I have prayed for you, that your faith will not fail in Jesus' name. Say Amen!

Remember it's only those who have ever gone through the Jordan, who can pick up stones for memorial. If you haven't passed somewhere you will have nothing to be remembered about. Great people are made by great challenges. Don't fear challenges but instead use them to help you to achieve greatness, putting into consideration that all remarkable people in history were made great by challenges.

CHAPTER 4 - MAN OF DESTINY

In the story of the Good Samaritan, Jesus talks about this man who was coming from Jerusalem to Jericho.

And Jesus answering said, A certain man went down from Jerusalem to Jericho, and fell among thieves, which stripped him of his raiment, and wounded him, and departed, leaving him half dead. Luke 10:30 (KJV)

Much has been written about the Good Samaritan but I want us to see the story in a new way as we focus on the man who was attacked on the way to Jericho. We shall call him a man of destiny.

Know where you are coming from and where you are going to

I want you to note something here. Firstly, Jesus does not give us the name of the man, instead he calls him a *"certain man."* He knew that it was not important for us to know the name of this man. If Jesus had given the man a name it would have excluded us from the story. The story isn't to be centred on him alone. For him to be an example to us, he has to be anonymous. Names can change along the way in life. Abram can become Abraham; Sarai can become Sarah; Jacob the man can become Israel the nation and Saul the persecutor of the Way can become Apostle Paul servant of the Lord Jesus Christ.

Secondly, Jesus doesn't tell us why this man was leaving Jerusalem for Jericho, whether he had problems in Jerusalem, or if he was running from debts or just shifting from Jerusalem; we don't know why he left Jerusalem.

Thirdly, why was he going to Jericho? Jesus doesn't give us the reason why he left Jerusalem and was going to Jericho. We do not know whether he was going for shopping or visiting friends or looking for a job or going to settle there. Jesus saw that all this is unimportant to us. One thing that was extremely important to Jesus was to tell us the place where this man was coming from and the place where this man was going to. He was coming from Jerusalem and going to Jericho. These two places are mentioned by name. This means that anyone who desires to live a victorious life on earth must know these two places: You must know where you are coming from and where you are going, in order to overcome what you will go through along the way.

God respects these two places so much. Even when he introduces Himself to us, he says, I am the First and the Last, I am the beginning and the end. I am the Alpha and the Omega. Think about the significance of that.

Even when he was delivering the children of Israel out of bondage, He told them I am taking you out of Egypt and taking you to Canaan. God may decide not to tell you of the Red Sea that you will meet on the way, or the desert and the challenges that you will face, yet He knows it all but He will never fail to tell you where you are coming from and where you are going to.

Show me anyone who is a failure in everything he does and I will show you someone who doesn't know where is coming from and where is going to. Distance is measured by determining with and from the beginning point to the ending point. Those who know where they began from will always know the distance they are remaining with to reach their destination.

The question I have for you now is, do you know where you are coming from and where you are going to? Can you testify about the distance you have covered already? Do you know the distance you are remaining with until you reach your destination? The reason why Jesus overcame his enemies is because he knew these two places in his life. He says in the Scriptures:

"Jesus answered and said unto them, Though I bear record of myself, yet my record is true: for I know whence I came, and whither I go; but ye cannot tell whence I come, and whither I go." John 8:14 (KJV)

God expects of you alone, all by yourself, as you listen to His voice and obey it to have a revelation of your destiny without waiting for others to be telling you what they think about you and your future.

Many people even go to the extent of asking: When you look at me what do you think? What do you see? Can I be married? Can I make it in this life? Can I do well in business? Then you wait for their answers to determine your next step. Ladies and gentlemen, you must have your personal stand and your personal revelation about your destiny. Jesus says, "I know" not, "we know". You must get to a level of knowing how to stand for what you know. What others know cannot determine your destiny until you yourself let it. It has to be what you know, and not what they know.

Jesus told them: *"But ye cannot tell whence I come, and whither I go."* But do you want to tell me that they had nothing to tell? Of course, they had a lot to tell but Jesus couldn't let them. When Jesus tells them "you cannot tell…" he is simply telling them to keep their opinions to themselves. They cannot determine my next level. I have no room for them. I have enough for myself. I don't need anyone's guess work about me.

The reason why most people are hurt is because they have opened up a big door for people to practise their opinions on them. The time you choose to close that door is the time that you will stop being a victim of other people's thoughts.

Let me give you an example: When you are taking a flight, the pilot alone can talk to the passengers anytime he feels like it and there is no passenger who has access to talk to the pilot at any time. No passenger can determine the speed of the plane, the altitude it flies at or the direction it takes. Everything is determined by the pilot alone. In the same way, God wants to have a monopoly on our thoughts and train us to listen only to His voice where it concerns our destiny, not to the voices of those who will distract or delay or destroy what God has placed upon our lives.

Destiny is Determined by a Resolute Mind

Destiny is determined by a resolute mind. The mind determined to achieve a certain goal will always be attracted to the like mind made up for the similar goal. Two cannot move together unless they are in agreement. Stop hooking up with people who cannot see what you see and talking with the people who cannot talk the same language of positivity as you.

Many people who had a great destiny have been side-tracked and blocked by people whom they called "friends" and yet they don't go the same direction with them. May the Lord open your spiritual eyes to see these people even before they come close to you. May you see them from far and avoid them. Let all their negative plans against your life fail, and let only the plans of God for your life succeed. May you achieve your goals in Jesus' name.

CHAPTER 5 - TAKE A STEP OF FAITH

This "certain man" that Jesus talks about, who was coming from Jerusalem saw Jericho when he was still in Jerusalem and he decided to go for what he saw. He was a man intent on pursuing his personal destiny.

There are numerous people that I am talking to right now who have seen many things in their life, things that are supposed to be theirs but they are not doing anything about it. What I believe is that this man could not have left Jerusalem for Jericho if Jerusalem was better than Jericho. In the context of this particular story he was a wise man who saw Jericho as a better circumstance for him than Jerusalem.

He saw greater opportunities in Jericho than Jerusalem; an improved way of living in Jericho. I know he spoke to himself and said, "I can live better in Jericho, I can have a better house, I can own superior properties, my children can study in the best schools; I can drive a good car. My life will be far better in Jericho than here in Jerusalem."

You see no one who is wise can begin a journey that is not profitable in some way. You cannot pursue something that is not adding value to your profile. Profile without profit is nothing.

Our God believes in profit. He is a God of profit. The first message he gave to man after creation was *"be fruitful ..."* that's profit! That is why anyone who believes in God, his/her main agenda in all that he/she does is to have profit and live a fruitful life that glorifies God. Ask yourself in whatever you do, does it profit you or does it profit the people around you? If the answer is no then you are wasting your time and energy.

In Matthew 25:14-30 Jesus talks about a man who went into a far country and who left his goods to three of his servants. Two of them did well because they gave him profit when he came back by investing the master's resources wisely. However, the last of the three men did not and this is what his master said to him on his return:

"His lord answered and said unto him, Thou wicked and slothful servant, thou knewest that I reap where I sowed not and gather where I have not strawed: Thou oughtest therefore to have put my money to the exchangers, and then at my coming I should have received mine own with usury [profit]*."
Matthew 25:26-27
*Emphasis mine

The biggest problem that the master and the servant have here is profit. How can I give you money and you fail to get profit out of it? The spiritual principle is this: How can God give you such a gift and you fail to get profit out of it? I am speaking here firstly of being fruitful with what God has given to you, not only in a financial capacity but also in a spiritual capacity. We have many people today whom God has given real gifts, real treasure but they are sitting doing nothing with what the Lord has entrusted to them. I came to tell you to rise up now and take a step of faith. You can do something about it. You can develop that talent. Get some profit out of it and bring joy to the Master!

In every one of us God has put untold talents and treasures that can profit in so many ways. Let the world know what you have. There is something that you alone can do in this whole world and you are the only one who can do it best. Do something about it. Take a step now.

The bible describes the servant who made no profit as "wicked." The master said, *"Thou wicked and slothful servant."* I looked at this word wicked and I said to myself, it is a big word. It is used for people who are killers, witches, robbers and those who are truly debase and wicked. I asked myself, how could the Lord ascribe such a word to a man like this? Then I came to understand that the Lord has given a talent, gift, calling and treasure of diverse kinds to mankind and people have buried it and made a decision to kill it. They have become killers of vision and he/she has killed the gift/talent that God has given to them. Therefore they are considered "wicked" in the context of not being a wise steward of what God has entrusted to them.

Why should you be "wicked" in your generation? Rise up and do something. When I hear how much professional football players earn each week it inspires me to ask myself is there anything else on earth that can pay more than a talent used to its optimum ability? Look at how many people gather to watch them play football. Stadiums are filled to capacity and the whole world is watching on TV. This is just one of the millions of talents that God has deposited in human beings. You have your talent as well and your talent has the potential to put the world on stand to watch you rise and excel in your particular area of gifting and calling. Remember you have to profit your generation. If you can only see more profit in Jericho than in Jerusalem where you are now, then the journey must begin.

Focusing Beyond

We might ask what did Jericho represent to this man when he was still in Jerusalem?

- Jericho was his vision
- Jericho was his dream
- Jericho was his goal
- Jericho was his target
- Jericho was his focus
- Jericho was his promise
- Jericho was his prophecy

Do you have a place in your near future you can call "Jericho" that is the centre of your focus, the purpose of your drive, the place that causes you to be restless for change every time you think about it?

This man saw Jericho when he was still in Jerusalem. I know I am talking to someone here who is still in a certain "Jerusalem", somewhere we can describe as a place where we are transitioning from into a new stage of destiny. Listen to what I came to tell you, it doesn't matter the kind of life you are living in that Jerusalem, just open your eyes and see Jericho. Speak to yourself and say, "I am not dying here. This is not my ending place but a beginning place. I am coming out of this and I am going somewhere. I can see a better life ahead of me. The best is yet to come!"

Let me prophesy to you right now. Many of your people died in that Jerusalem but you are not going to die there. You are coming out of it in Jesus' name. A new journey is beginning with you. A new chapter is opening around you. A new place is calling on your name. I see you rising up to the next level. Something that has never taken place in your entire family is going to begin with you very soon in Jesus' name.

Don't compare yourself with those who failed. You shall not fail like them. Your name shall be remembered among those who were the first to succeed in your family. Rise up and take a step, Jericho is calling you. Always remember, successful people were not born successful. Winners had a race to run. Conquerors had a battle to fight. Those on top had stairs to climb. Those in palaces had prisons they went through before reaching a place of high status. Those who married daughters of kings had Goliaths to fight. The steps that they took to face their challenges bore fruits in their lives, leaving great history behind them and creating powerful legacy for future generations to be blessed. These are our grandfathers of the faith. We learn from them and they are our examples. Their God is our God as well.

Together with all of them being our examples, how can we come out as failures? We must rise up and take every step possible to achieve our goals. This journey must begin, continue and reach its destination and along the way it cannot fail to bring forth Kingdom profit and fruits.

Ask yourself a question, how can you see what you cannot see? You must learn to focus beyond what you can see in your present circumstances and concentrate instead on the great faith promises that God has for you in the future. You can rise up and take that first step towards your goals and I promise you, you will see how it will change your entire life. Don't fear to fight those battles. You are not the first one to fight and you will not be the last. You will not fail, just trust in God. All those who fought in the name of God, had all the victory and you will have all the victory as well. Don't be afraid to rise up and take a step. Come out of that Jerusalem.

CHAPTER 6 - CHALLENGES ON THE WAY TO YOUR DESTINY

And Jesus answering said, A certain man went down from Jerusalem to Jericho, and fell among thieves, which stripped him of his raiment, and wounded him, and departed, leaving him half dead." Luke 10:30 (KJV)

This certain man Jesus talked about in this story began his journey very well from Jerusalem leading to Jericho. But we see what happened to him - on the way he fell among thieves. What surprises me is that in Jerusalem, these thieves were not there, neither were they in Jericho but they were found "on the way". These thieves cannot steal or attack anyone who is not travelling. If you are in your Jerusalem, you can't see them. They are on the way. And you might ask yourself: who are these thieves who are on my way? For you to identify who they are, you must first identify what they do. Jesus said, they stripped him of his raiment, and wounded him and departed, leaving him half dead.

Oh okay, I can now know who they are. When I see anyone or anything coming in my way to strip me naked and wound me and leave half dead, I will not wait for any prophet to prophesy to me that "those are the thieves says the Lord." I will automatically know them. These are the enemies of my progress. You can also call them challenges or obstacles or oppositions or hindrances or roadblocks or afflictions, desolations or trauma.

You cannot encounter these if there is no journey you have begun in your life. I have always heard people say, "Before I began this thing I was very okay but after I began, so many challenges have risen up." Yes, it's true, because there is a journey that has begun in your life, so thieves must be there on the way.

It cannot rain without first of all showing clouds covering the sky as a sign that it is about to rain. So also the sign that shows that you are going somewhere are the enemies that rise up against your life. They don't oppose stagnant people. They talk against those that are moving.

They don't know where you are coming from and where you are going. You just met at college, or at the rental apartment or you just met them in the church. After knowing you for a year or two they now tend to think they know you so much. Can you imagine? Thinking that two years can determine how your entire life should be like? Two years is not an expression of your life in totality.

Your destiny is not measured by what you have been through the past two years. No. Even Joseph who was in prison for more than two years ended up as the first Prime Minister of Egypt. It is not all about where you are right now, but where you are going after there. Keep your focus on your destination and not on the journey. The journey will raise up questions that you will not have answers for until you get to your destination.

You don't have to know everything on the way. You just need to know much about your destiny potential. Use your challenges as wake-up calls, to keep you awake all the way. Let every tension keep you spiritually alert and attentive. Let no one deceive you that it shall be easy for you on the way. No, it won't. From the very beginning, people hate dreamers. But now what will the dreamers do? Should they stop dreaming? Do dreamers prepare what to dream? No. Dreams don't *come from* dreamers, but only *come to* dreamers. God is the only one who gives dreams to dreamers. That is why the same God who gave a dream to a dreamer will always fight for the dreamer until his or her dream comes to pass. Dreamers can't just die on the way.

The man was stripped of his raiment, wounded and left half dead. He was half dead, which means there must be another "half" help that God will always leave for himself to provide for us. No one on earth has a full authority over your life. No one. They can only do half. Then God will come in for the full pack.

So many people today are stripped naked. The enemy has taken their garment (raiment). This garment represents glory and identity and position. Jesus is trying to teach us that we shouldn't expect to dress well when we are still on the way. Let us forget about titles and position until we get to our destination. But let me encourage you:

- When they begin to hate you as a dreamer, don't hate yourself
- When they beat you, don't beat yourself up
- When they call you names, don't' call yourself names

Don't give up on your future destiny because of opposition that you met on the way.

The Word You Believe in Will Create the World You Live In

The number of those that are wounded is big, crying over wounds that no man can heal. Everybody they try to run to for help seems not to understand them well. They only give advice such as: Just forget that journey, seems like God is not in it. If God is the one who told you, why should he allow you to go through all that? Are you sure you are not just being driven by your instincts? I mean they can talk to you like that until you feel like it's not God. But listen to me, don't allow people to cause you to doubt God. They can advise you wrongly because they don't want to help you.

Simply because they cannot understand what you are doing doesn't necessarily mean that what you are doing is wrong. What God is doing in your life doesn't need man's approval to be true. The God who started a good work in you, will surely bring it to accomplishment. Put your trust in God, Knowing that he who spoke, knows how it shall happen. Don't allow people's opinions to drive you crazy. Stick to the word of God. The word you believe in will create the world you will live in.

People's contributions in your life on the way to your destiny might be negative, but don't let that be a problem to you. Negative contributions of people can lead us to positive destinations in God. As you pass through the sea there are inevitably winds and storms. On the road there will always be potholes and roadblocks and enemies. And even if you use air transport there is often a lot of turbulence along the way. Every journey has challenges and blessings.

Every way to your destiny will always have a lot of challenges but the good news I have for you is that He who began it all will finish it. God promised that:

But now thus saith the Lord that created thee, O Jacob, and he that formed thee, O Israel, Fear not: for I have redeemed thee, I have called thee by thy name; thou art mine.

When thou passest through the waters, I will be with thee; And through the rivers, they shall not overflow thee: when thou walkest through the fire, thou shalt not be burned: Neither shall the flame kindle upon thee." Isaiah 43:1-2 (KJV)

This is an assurance that God gave to us who believe in him, that he shall be with us. But remember he is telling us that the journey will have a lot of challenges. But in all of those God will be with us throughout.

I have heard so many quoting this Scripture, with an understanding that God will be with them when they are seated in deep waters, or seated in flames of fire or seated in challenges. But I want to tell you, that God is not addressing those that are stationary and seated because verse 2 says, *"when thou passest through the waters ..."* He is talking to those who are "passing through" which means they are on a journey going somewhere, they are not stagnant and seated down in the midst of their circumstances because they have come to realise they have a destiny in their life. They will advance through adversity and pass on through to the promises of God for their lives.

Stop sitting in your troubles and expecting God to be with you. Move on regardless of all that you are going through. The journey must not stop. I like the way so many people make positive confessions without knowing it. They say, "You don't know what I am going through. Pastor, you don't understand what I am going through." I like the phrase, "going through." They always cry over issues that they are "going through." Why should you cry? Go through! Why should someone else know what you are going through? You're not there to say. Go through, tomorrow you will be over to the other side.

The reason why many people can't get anywhere in life is because they have diverted their attention from their destinations to the circumstances they are going through. Immediately you allow yourself to become a victim of circumstances, you will not get anywhere in this life. Winners over circumstances are the achievers of destinies.

How many people do we have today who are struggling with inner wounds? They dress well and move on the streets and the whole world thinks that they are okay, yet inside they are wounded; wounded in their marriage but still trusting God for a certain help. Wounded in their businesses, but believing God for breakthrough. You look at them and you think everything is ok with them, yet they know what they are passing through. If everyone was to open up and tell the truth of the journey they are on, you would be shocked by all the stories you might hear.

Those who have imagined themselves to be winners have decided to stick to the journey regardless of anything that might rise up to meet them on the way. Don't even try to think that you are the only one facing those challenges on the way alone. Everyone faces them, but the thing that makes a difference is how you choose to respond to them. You must understand that facing difficulties doesn't mean that it's the end of the journey for you. Challenges will usher you into the next stage of your destiny. They will become a stepping stone on your journey.

The thieves took everything that this man of destiny owned. They took his money, they took his horse, his clothes, all his possessions – everything that he had and they beat him up and wounded him and left him half-dead and then they went on their way.

These thieves' intention was to make sure that they had taken everything from him and probably leave him for dead. But what amazes me is that the very place where they found him, is the exact place where they left him. You see thieves may come and God will allow them to take everything you have but they will never rob you of your journey and they cannot take you back to where you came from. Where they met you is where they will leave you. They have no power to take you back to where you began from.

If they had wanted to finish him they should have carried him back to Jerusalem. But the robbers on the road to Jericho did not have that ability and neither do the robbers who will meet you on your journey today. God will not allow them to do that so don't worry about them. They can only beat you and take what you have but they cannot take you backwards to where you have come from.

What blesses me is that just as Joseph's brothers took his coat of many colours they could not take his mantle. Thieves can take your "coat of many colours" but they cannot take your God-dreams out of you. And remember that the dreams that they can't take, will bring back the coat of many colours. Isn't that powerful?

Your destiny is still intact. Your dreams are still with you. You cannot lose anything as far as your destiny is concerned. You might not be left with anything right now but remember you are still a dreamer.

- Working as a slave but still a dreamer
- Having nowhere to stay but still dreaming
- No one wants to associate with you but don't worry about them. Continue with your dreams. Your dreams will bring back everything the thieves took from you. A dreamer with God's help will never be a loser.
-

I have met people who want to die, tragically even others have committed suicide because of losing what they had. That is the total lie of the devil. Because if you managed to get something, it means that you have that ability within you to achieve. So even if it's taken away from you temporarily, you can bounce back again. What is stolen is only the product; importantly the process that is making you a man or woman of destiny is still there. You can continue in your process regardless of what the thieves thought they had taken from you.

- You are not a produce but a producer
- You are not a product but a processor
- You are not an imitator but an initiator
- You are not a problem but a pioneer
- You are not a consumer but a manufacturer
- You are a source!

In Uganda we say that you are a log of Cassava plantation, meaning everywhere they throw you, you can germinate.

Oh yes! You have the ability to germinate anywhere in this world. You cannot fail in this life. If God is for you, who can be against you. Even if they lift you now and they throw you in a country where there is no one you know, within three months you will be already germinating.

I want you to know that the ability to succeed anywhere is within you. Don't allow those thieves to make you think that you are a failure because they have taken all that you had. Many people look at what has happened to you and they come up with their own interpretations but don't be moved by them. These days they might say that you have a curse or that you are bewitched. That's what they think but remember what God thinks about you is not the same.

Give yourself time. Don't rush over issues. Relax yourself. Take one step at a time. Before they come to know it, you will be coming out a winner and the same people who doubted your call will be helping you to testify about what God will have done in your life.

Always understand that there is no wound caused by a man that God cannot heal. All those wounds in you, God will heal them and the journey shall continue. Where you are now is not the end of the journey.

What have you lost? What has been taken away from you? What is the reaction of your friends about it? How do you feel about it? Whom do you think was responsible for your loss? The answers to these questions have been the main focus of so many people who are wounded on the way to fulfilment of their destinies. But I want you to be very careful about this because you might end up trying to find these answers and waste your time for nothing. Even if you find the answers they will not help you to achieve anything. What you need is just to trust God for a new arising. Otherwise you cannot expect that you will first get those answers and then be able to rise up. Please just understand that challenges will always be there to anyone who is going somewhere in life.

CHAPTER 7 - STOP LIVING BY CHANCE

And by chance there came down a certain priest that way; and when he saw him, he passed by on the other side, And likewise a Levite, when he was at the place, came and looked on him, and passed by on the other side." Luke 10:31-32 (KJV)

Destiny is not achieved by chance. People who believe in chance are people who are not sure of their choices in life. Probability is what promotes chance. But when choice comes in, chance can't stand. This mentality of chance has caused many people to be disappointed in their life because they end up not getting what they thought chance could have given them.

Look at this man of destiny on the way to Jericho. When he was left bleeding and half dead, by chance there came a priest. Now if you live by chance you will think his salvation has come. But wait a little bit and see how this chance will pass him without even touching him.

The priest saw him very well and knew how much he was hurting but yet he passed him by on the other side, and likewise a Levite. 'These two chances passed him and nothing could work for him.

Not everybody who comes close to you has it in mind to help you. Stop thinking that that was your chance but maybe you didn't seize it well or if you had acted in a different way you might have had it. People will come up with stories of how you could have maximised that moment to get the attention of that priest or that Levite. But I want you to understand today some people came your way but they have nothing for you at all. They came to pass you by. Let them go. They can know your name, your problems, and your address for now but don't cling to them. They are just passing.

Many times we have a problem of letting people go out of our lives, yet if you don't allow them to go they might turn out to be more dangerous than those thieves and robbers who assailed the man on the road to Jericho. Simply because they have been your friends for a year or two doesn't mean they shall be your friends forever. Let them go. They are the wrong people who are occupying seats for the right ones. When you allow them to go, is the time when you shall see the right people coming.

Are you not tired of the pain they are increasing in your heart or life? You see it's better to bleed when they are not there at all than them being there and see you well and then just pass you by when you are in trouble and leave you like that. They cause you to have much more pain. You know they have the capacity to help you but they deliberately refuse to help you. It pains you more to have a rich uncle who passes you by. It pains you more to have a rich auntie who knows your problem and need but passes you by like you are dead already.

I am talking to people today who are in pains of being passed and left bleeding by people they thought could have been there to help them out of their challenges.

Questioning themselves:
- I have relatives who have all the money but how come they don't want to help me?
- Why do people just pass me by as if they don't see me?
- What's wrong with me?
- Do I have a spirit of hatred or rejection?

Such a situation can raise a lot of questions without proper answers but what I can say to you is allow them to go. Not all that come close to you have your help in mind. Forget those who are a hindrance and move on with your life.

I want you to know that most people don't want to associate with those who have problems and needs. When you are hurting and bleeding, don't expect to have many friends.

When you are still finding your way, very few want to identify with you. When your clothes and cars and properties are taken no one says, "we went to school together" or, "we came from the same village" with him/her. When you are in debt, chased out from your office or struggling with life no one comes close to you. They see you and pass by on the other side.

But I have very good news for you – Jesus will never allow you to remain in the condition in which He found you or permit you to stay bound up in the situation in which the robbers left you. He is faithful to lift you up from your situation. He will send a Good Samaritan who can look at you and see a man or woman of destiny going somewhere in life. Yes, God will send a Good Samaritan - a destiny builder and destiny helper who will help you to heal and get on the way to fulfilment of God's plans for your life.

Christ has gladly paid the price unconditionally and without demand to assist in your healing and restoration. Along the way He will send a Good Samaritan who will not make any demand upon you for recompense so that you will reach your Jericho as a man or woman of destiny! God bless you in your journey.

AUTHOR BIOGRAPHY: ABOUT STEPHEN KATO

"TWIN MINISTRY – NEW DESTINY MINISTRIES"

Isaiah 43:18-19 (NLT)
18 "But forget all that--
it is nothing compared to what I am going to do.
19 For I am about to do something new.
See, I have already begun! Do you not see it?
I will make a pathway through the wilderness.
I will create rivers in the dry wasteland.

IDENTIFYING GOD'S PEOPLE TO THE NEW DESTINY THAT GOD HAS FOR THEM

Stephen Kato along with his twin brother **Godfrey Waswa** are the Co-Founders and International Directors of *"Twin Ministry – New Destiny Ministries"* based in Kampala, Uganda, East Africa. *New Destiny Ministries* is a multi-cultural, multi-racial, Holy Spirit filled, Word-based cutting edge Kingdom apostolic ministry. It has global influence and has made a powerful impact through an extensive relational network in many nations including Uganda, Tanzania, Kenya, Zambia; London, Birmingham (UK); Canada and numerous states throughout the USA. They also pastor a church called New Destiny Christian Centre in Kamuli, Uganda.

The twins were radically saved in 1985 and since that time have been used by God in spreading the Gospel message of hope and restoration to the weary, to sinners, to saints and to servants of God alike. *New Destiny Ministries* regularly conduct revival and restoration meetings, leadership gatherings, seminars and crusades with which they spread the Gospel of Jesus Christ and the message that God has put upon their hearts. They work with many different churches, organisations, ministries and business people to contribute to the development of God's people and are committed to improving living conditions of humanity, to discipling God's people and to building His church. The ministry has a church plant in Kamuli, with exciting plans for a brand new mega-church plant in Kampala in 2015.

New Destiny Ministries have an extensive global radio and developing TV ministries.

Both *Kato* and *Waswa* are sought after international teachers and preachers of the Word of God. They are men of integrity and humility whose apostolic ministries have been marked with signs and wonders following to the glory of God. *Kato* operates in a powerful breakthrough anointing especially in the area of faith miracles and finances. *Waswa* operates in a powerful breakthrough anointing in the area of teaching on God's government.

They can be contacted via:
www.twinministry.weebly.com katotwin.sk@gmail.com twinministries@yahoo.com
P.O.Box 71 Kamuli Uganda, East Africa
Stephen Kato: +256 782 611 077 (Uganda); Godfrey Waswa: +256 782 654 711 (Uganda)

OTHER BOOKS BY STEPHEN KATO

COMING VERY SOON ....

"Believe Only"
 - Jesus and Jairus

"Chosen to be Blessed"
-Twin Ministry

"God's Language"
– the Power of Unity

"It is a Journey"
– Surviving Storms

"Divine Visitation"
– Getting out of Your Basket